A-Minute-A-Day
Mental Maths

2019 US Edition

42 Photocopiable One Minute Challenges
to Improve Mental Maths Skills

A Teacher Timesaver by Sheila Crompton

DEBRICH PUBLISHING

2019
PUBLISHED BY DEBRICH PUBLISHING, LOCHSIDE FARM,
SANQUHAR, DUMFRIESSHIRE. DG4 6EW.

3rd Edition © DEBRICH PUBLISHING 2019

A catalogue record of this book has been lodged and is available from the
British Library.

ISBN 978-0-9536023-9-1

WHAT IS A MINUTE A DAY?

A-MINUTE-A-DAY is a series of 3 books, which aim to improve basic reading and mental maths skills, in a challenging yet fun way.

Each book contains a number of photocopiable games, each focussing upon specific groups of letters, words or numbers.

The aim of each game is for the student to give as many correct verbal answers as possible within 1 minute. *No writing skills are required.*

Each page or worksheet can be used repeatedly by the student for practice both in school and at home, and progress assessed by the teacher in just A-MINUTE-A-DAY.

WHY A-MINUTE-A-DAY?

A-MINUTE-A-DAY has at its roots, a method known as *precision teaching,* which, since its inception in 1964, has been adopted by an ever increasing number of teachers, and its proven success in both mainstream and special needs education is indisputable.

The value of precision teaching lies in identifying a specific area of need for a particular child, followed by a daily period of teaching, testing and evaluating progress.

Normally, this process can take around 10-15 minutes of completely undivided attention for a particular child. Whilst this can be considered a short enough period to offer any child, for a teacher without ancillary support and with multiple children requiring similar help, it can often be impossible to achieve.

A-MINUTE-A-DAY offers a new methodology, which enables teachers to offer their students tailored systematic practice and monitoring of progress on a daily basis, whilst drastically reducing the amount of teacher involvement.

A-MINUTE-A-DAY MENTAL MATHS

There has long been concern amongst teachers about the dangers of over-dependence by children upon aids such as calculators, which are frequently relied upon for even the most basic of calculations.

Educators have sought to redress this problem by encouraging the learning by rote of multiplication tables and the solving of simple problems, which encourage mental dexterity.

A-MINUTE-A-DAY MENTAL MATHS fully supports this approach. It focuses upon basic skills, which, when assimilated, will free the child to extend his/her mathematical thinking, and provide a firm foundation upon which all future mathematical work may be based.

KEY FEATURES OF A-MINUTE-A-DAY

ENCOURAGES PARENTAL INVOLVEMENT

So many teachers battle stoically on, alone, and yet there is a vast and frequently untapped source of support in the form of parents and family who are invariably eager and capable of participating in their child's education.

FUN - YET CHALLENGING. EVERY CHILD CAN ENJOY SUCCESS.

Parents want their children to learn, so let us show them how they can help, but LET IT BE FUN, not with tedious lists, but with games. Above all, let us ensure that homework at Primary level is a shared experience for parent and child.

SAVES HOURS OF HOMEWORK PREPARATION AND MARKING

Often, there is insufficient time to set homework on a regular basis for primary children, and still less time to check it. If, therefore, there is some way in which teachers could direct parents to an area of need for their child, which they would practise for no more than 10 minutes a night, all that is required of the teacher, is **A-MINUTE-A-DAY** to monitor the child's progress.

IMPROVEMENT IS MEASURABLE AND EASILY UNDERSTOOD BY THE CHILD

Children love competition - provided that the pressure is not too great. Let them compete against themselves. If they can answer six questions one night, make sure they can answer eight the next, and so on...It does not matter where you begin, it's how much you improve that counts. Often the slowest children are able to enjoy the most success, because they have the room for the greatest improvement.

SPEED + ACCURACY = FLUENCY.

Each game requires the child to give 30 correct verbal responses within 1 minute. This gives adequate opportunity for accurate responses. There is little value in encouraging speed at the expense of accuracy. As the child becomes more skilful, and the first goal is achieved, the time limit may be reduced. For most of the games, a time limit of thirty seconds should not be beyond the ability of the average child.

BLANK GAMES TO SUPPORT FURTHER MENTAL MATHS WORK

Included at the end of the book are three content free games, which may be used by the teacher to create additional mental maths questions to suit an individual child, or to offer a game with high repetition for children who learn more slowly.

Sheila Crompton 2019

A-Minute-A-Day MENTAL MATHS (US)
CONTENTS

	Counting Objects		
1	Birthday		up to 6
2	Ladybird		up to 10
3	Dominoes		up to 12
	Number Recognition		
4	Match		up to 11
5	Balloons		up to 20
6	Soldiers		up to 30
	Addition		
7	Magnetic Fishing		up to 10
8	Fireworks		up to 20
	Subtraction		
9	Dice		from 7
10	Skittles		from 10
11	Chocolate Beans		from 20
12	Ducks		between 0 and 10
13	Marbles		between 10 and 20
	Multiplication/division		
14	Letters		x 2
15	Blackbirds		x 3
16	Caterpillar		x 4
17	Flowers		x 5
18	Candy Store		x 6
19	Crocodile		x 7
20	Lighthouse		x 8
21	Umbrellas		x 9
22	Ski Race		x 10 and ÷ 10

A-Minute-A-Day MENTAL MATHS (US)

Division cont..

23	Mary	÷2
24	Fish	÷3
25	Plums	÷4
26	Homework	÷5
27	Tunnel	÷6
28	Socks	÷7
29	Eggs	÷8
30	Bins	÷9

Time

31	Time	o'clock/half past
32	Alarm	quarter to/past
33	Watch	5 to/past 10 to/past
34	Meg	20 to/past 25 to/past

Money

35	Lunch	addition to 25c
36	Piggy Bank	addition to 50c
37	School Outing	addition to $1
38	Change	change from 25c
39	Spends	change from 50c

Content free

40	Snakes and Ladders	
41	Skyscraper	
42	Downfall	

Birthday

It is Pam's birthday.
She has come for her cake.
Can you help her to find it?

Count the candles on every cake.
Hurry! The party begins in 1 minute.

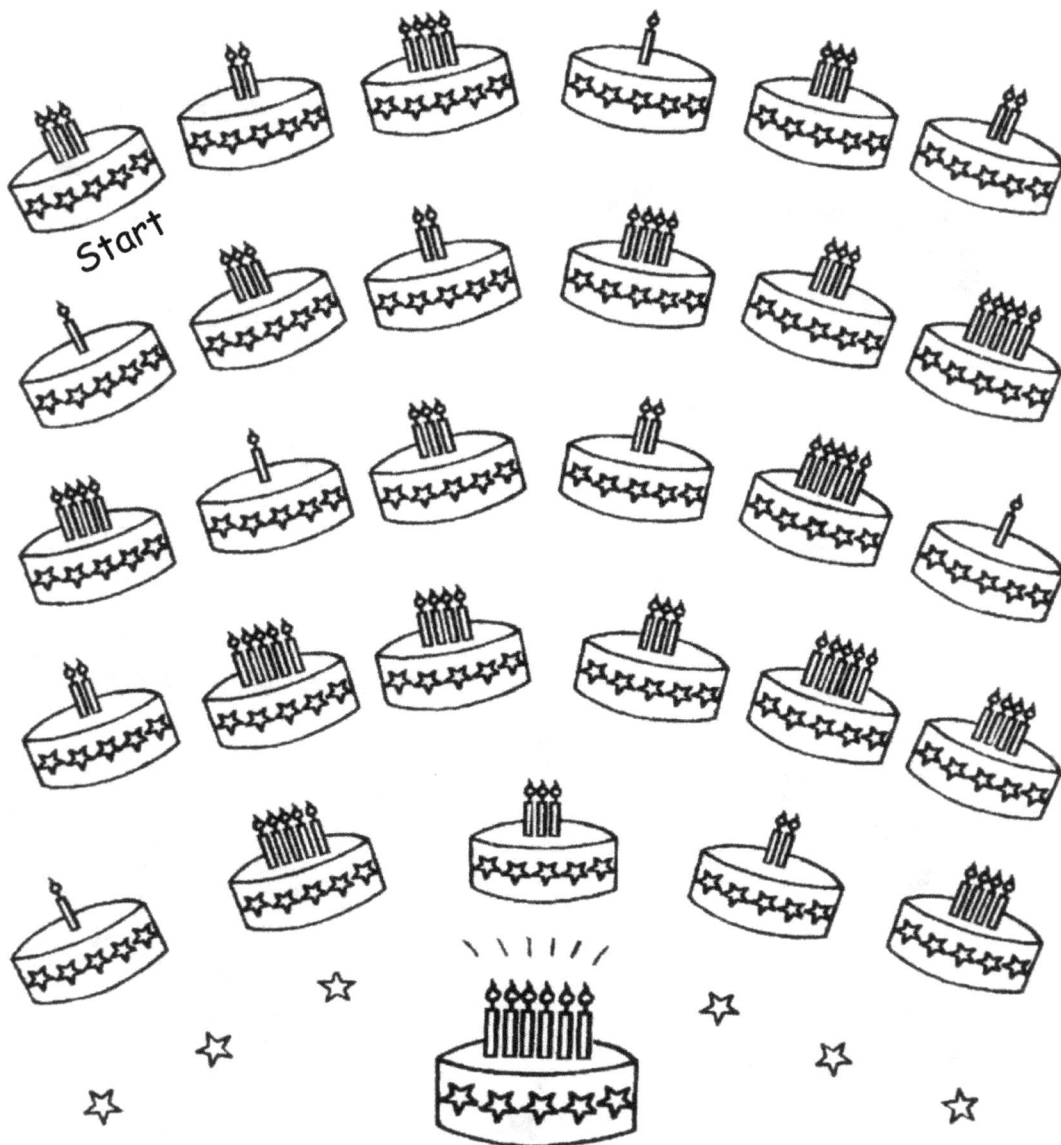

Start

A-Minute-A-Day – Debrich Publishing – Copyright 2019

Practice every day.   Write your score on the back.   1

Ladybird

"Ladybird, ladybird, fly away home ...."

The ladybirds have different numbers of spots.
Can you count them all before they fly away?

Start

You have 1 minute to try.

Practice every day.

Write your score on the back

Dominoes

John is adding the spots on each domino.
He can do it in 1 minute. Can you beat him?

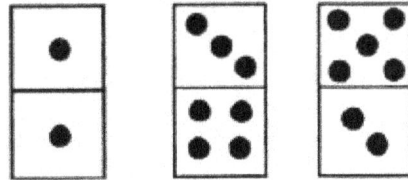

"5"

Start

Well
done!

A-Minute-A-Day - Debrich Publishing - Copyright 2019

Practice every day.   Write your score on the back   3

Match

The players are late for the match.
Can you help them to find the right shirts,
by calling out the numbers?

Start

9　8　6　5　7　10

Hurry! The match starts in 1 minute.

4　5　2　11　3　8

8　10　1　3　9　4

Practice every day.

7　2　11　3　4　6

9　7　5　6　2　11

Finish !

Write your scores on the back

Balloon Race

It is a very windy day.
In just 1 minute, the balloons
will have blown away

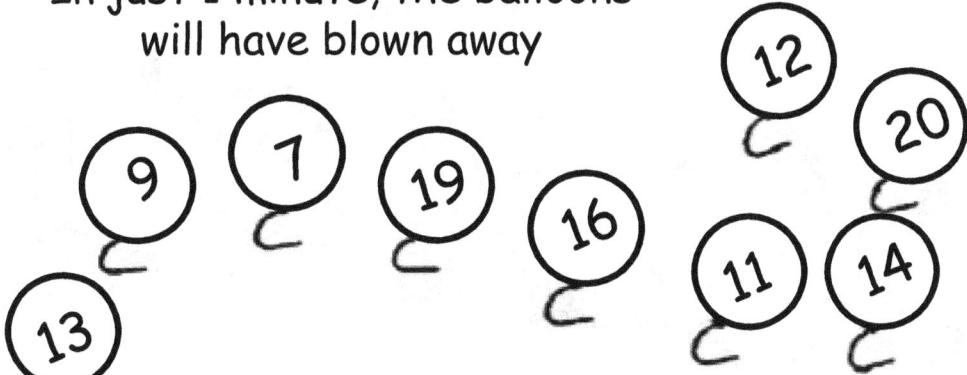

12

20

9   7   19

16

13   11   14

5

14   Can you read the numbers
         before they disappear?

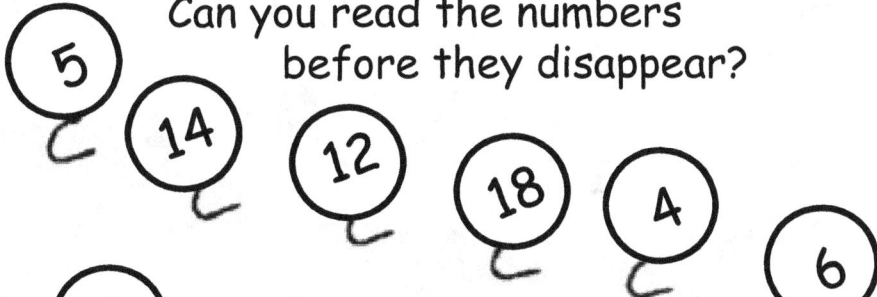

12

18   4

6

3   11
       2   Practice every day.

18   15   8

1   17

20

Write your scores on the back

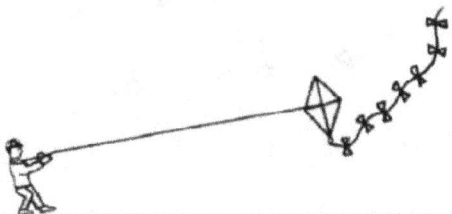

13   10   15   17

16
19

Start

Soldiers

Can you help John to put his soldiers in the right order?
Touch each soldier as you say its number.
Start at 1 and count up to 30

You have 1 minute to try.

Practice every day.

If you make a mistake,
you must start again!

Write your scores on the back.

Magnetic Fishing

You have 1 minute to catch as many fish as you can. You must not miss out any fish and you must answer each sum correctly.

3+4

start

5+5

4+6

2+5

8+1

1+4

5+2

2+7

3+3

3+5

2+4

1+7

6+2

0+10

4+4

4+5

1+6

5+4

1+9

3+6

2+6

1+9

4+2

3+2

1+5

3+7

6+3

10+0

2+3

2+8

Practice every day   Put your score on the back   7

A-Minute-A-Day - Debrich Publishing - Copyright 2019

Fireworks

In 1 minute, Pete's father
will light the fireworks

Can you answer all the questions
before they explode?

bang!

8 +7	12 +1	5 +6	15 +4	8 +3	10 +5	13 +5

18 +2	13 +2	4 +9	5 +8	12 +6	7 +4	11 +6	17 +2

3 +9	14 +5	6 +5	9 +5	4 +8	16 +2

9 +3

Start

13 +7	7 +8	11 +2	16 +4	10 +7	8 +4	16 +3	11 +6

Practice every day. Write your scores on the back.

8

A-Minute-A-Day – Debrich Publishing – Copyright 2019

Dice

Look at the number on top of a dice.
Look at the number on the bottom.
Add the two numbers together.

Do the same with the other opposite sides.
What do you notice?

Here is the top of another dice.
What number will be on the bottom?

Now guess the numbers on the bottom of these dice.
You have 1 minute to guess them all.

start

A-Minute-A-Day - Debrich Publishing - Copyright 2019

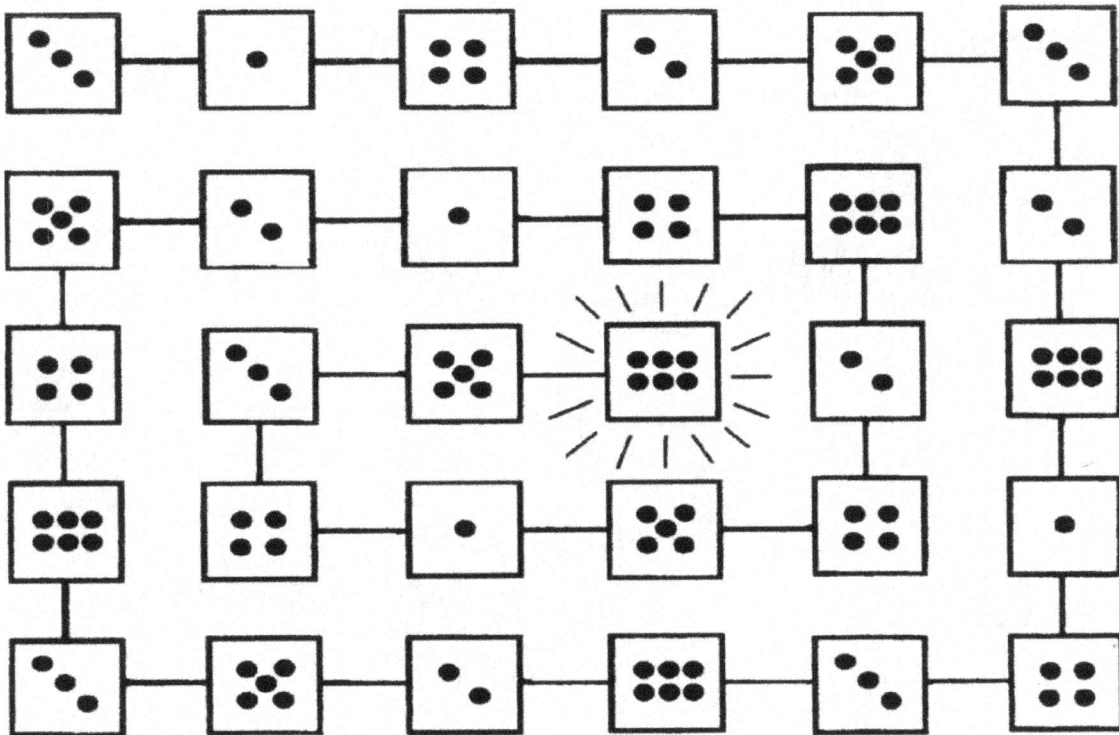

Practice every day.   Write your scores on the back.   9

Skittles

Sam tried to knock down 10 skittles
but 4 were still standing.
His score was 6.

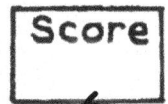

Score

He decided to practice hard.
Can you tell him how many he scored each time?

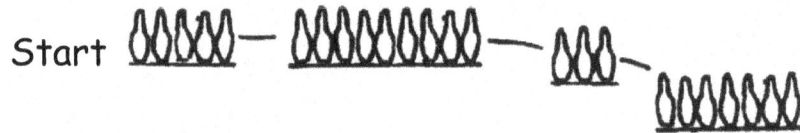

Start

Try to do them all in 1 minute.

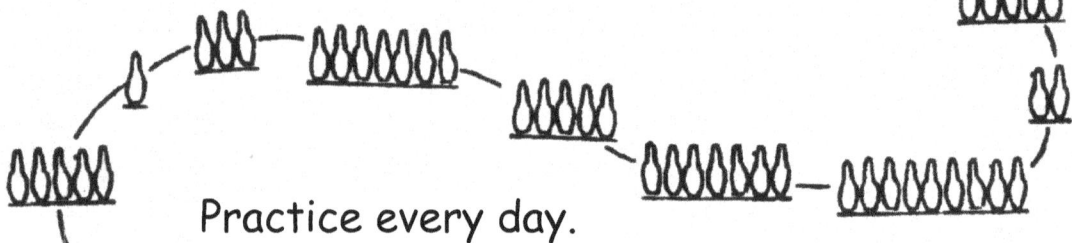

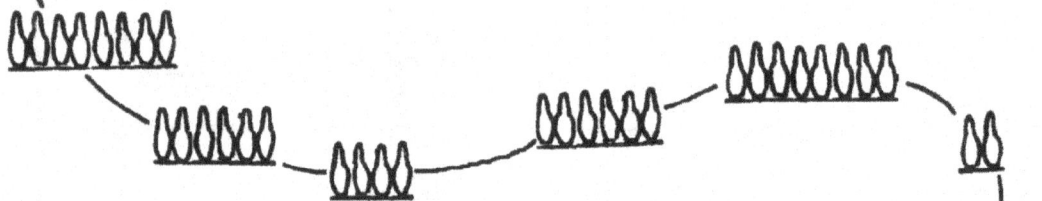

Practice every day.

Put your score on the back.

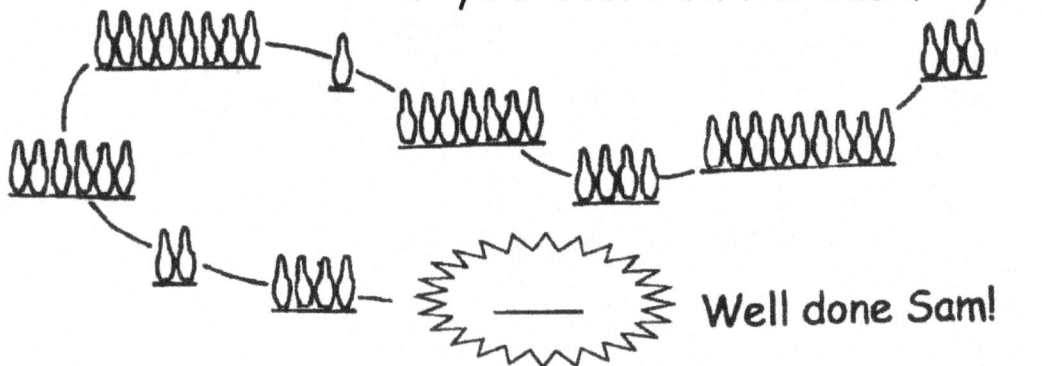

Well done Sam!

A-Minute-A-Day - Debrich Publishing - Copyright 2019

10

Chocolate Beans

There were 20 chocolate beans in every tube.
Can you say how many have been taken from each one?

Hurry! The children will be back in 1 minute
to eat all the rest.

Start

15 12 7 10 14

6 18 9 4 5

5 13

3 16 6 10

14 11 2 9 8 3

12 19

2 4 7 11 8 17

Practice every day.   Put your score on the back.

Ducks

Sue is having fun at the fair on the Hook-a-Duck stall.
She hopes to catch a number 5 duck and win a prize.

Can you tell her the number on
the bottom of each duck?

You have only 1 minute to try.

8-3
5

Start

| 7-4 | 10-1 | 9-5 | 6-5 | 6-4 |

| 8-6 | 8-2 | 7-6 | 9-1 | 10-0 |

| 10-3 | 8-4 | 10-2 | 7-1 | 9-7 |

| 9-3 | 8-5 | 9-2 | 8-7 | 7-3 |

| 8-1 | 7-5 | 9-6 | 10-4 | 5-3 |

| 9-4 | 9-0 | 6-2 | 10-7 | 8-0 |

Practice every day.   Write your score on the back.   12

Marbles

All of Jack's friends started with 20 marbles but
Jack is a very good player. He beat them all.
Try to guess how many they each had left.

Start 20-5   20-9   20-7   20-14   20-6

You have 1 minute to try.

20-10   20-5   20-3   20-6   20-15

20-4

20-7   20-4   20-11

20-12   20-16

Well done !   20-2   20-7

20-6   20-19   20-13

20-17   20-1   20-8

20-3

20-8   20-10   20-2   20-18   20-11

Practice every day.   Write your score on the back.   13

A-Minute-A-Day - Debrich Publishing - Copyright 2019

Letters

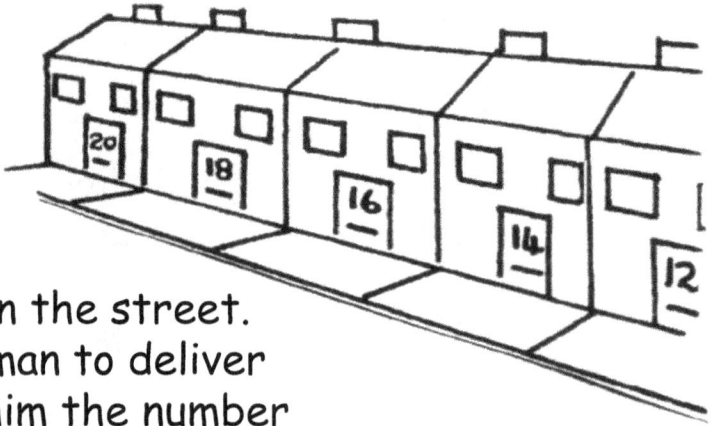

There are 20 houses in the street.
Can you help the postman to deliver
his letters by telling him the number
on each envelope.

See if you can do them all in 1 minute.

10x2	6x2	2x2	9x2	3x2
7x2	3x2	4x2	8x2	5x2
4x2	10x2	9x2	1x2	6x2
9x2	7x2	2x2	5x2	3x2
6x2	8x2	4x2	7x2	5x2
2x2	5x2	9x2	8x2	10x2

Practice every day.   Write your scores on the back.   14

A-Minute-A-Day - Debrich Publishing - Copyright 2019

♫ Blackbirds

"Sing a song of sixpence,
A pocket full of rye,
Four and twenty blackbirds
Baked in a pie .... "

Can you guess how many blackbirds are in each pie?
Hurry! The king will be here in 1 minute for his dinner.

Start

6x3   2x3   8x3
            7x3
9x3   3x3   7x3   4x3
            5x3
2x3   10x3
      4x3   8x3
                  10x3
7x3   1x3   7x3   2x3
                  9x3
9x3   8x3   5x3
            6x3   0x3
6x3   3x3
      4x3   5x3   8x3   10x3

If you make a mistake, you must go back to the start!
Practice every day. Write your score on the back.   15

Caterpillar

6x4

10x4

2x4

4x4

8x4

1x4

6x4

5x4

9x4

6x4

7x4

2x4

7x4

10x4

8x4

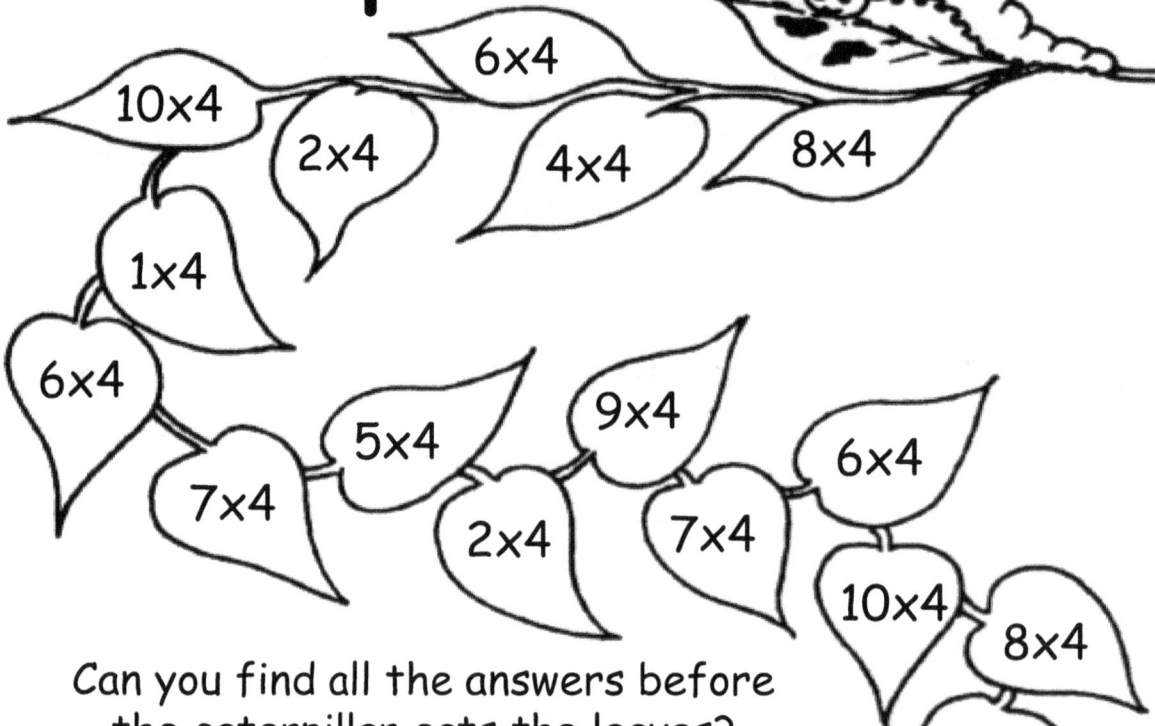

Can you find all the answers before
the caterpillar eats the leaves?

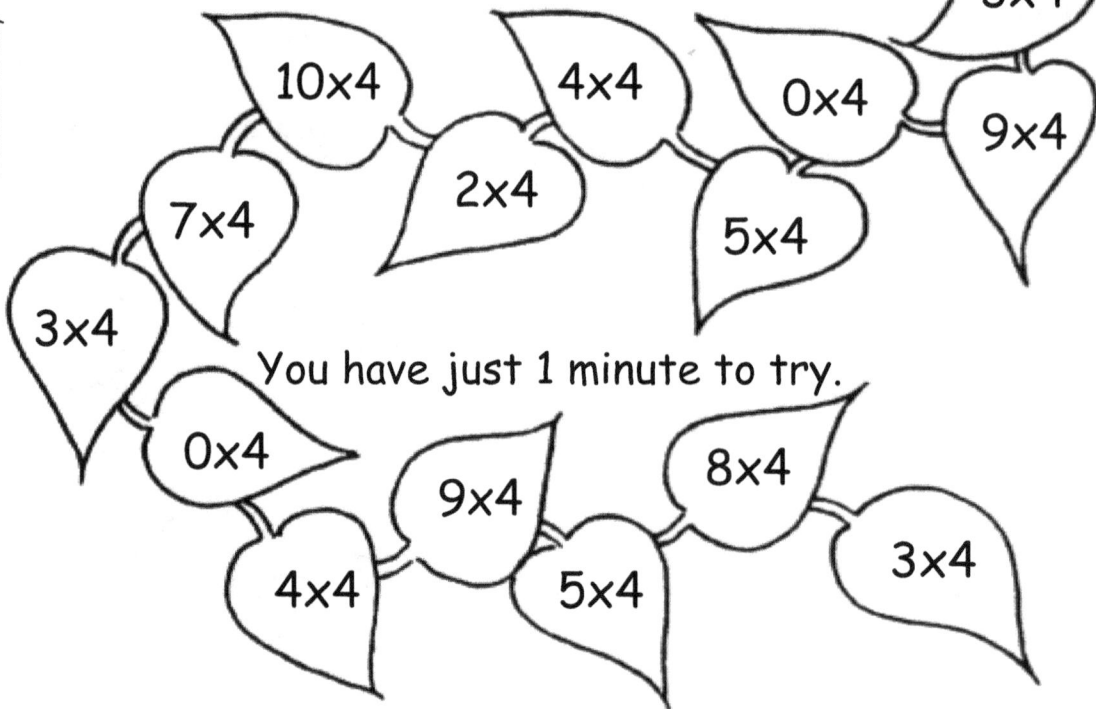

3x4

10x4

4x4

0x4

9x4

2x4

7x4

5x4

3x4

You have just 1 minute to try.

0x4

9x4

8x4

4x4

5x4

3x4

A-Minute-A-Day - Debrich Publishing - Copyright 2019

Practice every day. Write your score on the back.

16

Flowers

Every flower has 5 petals.
Can you guess the number
of petals in each pot?

5 petals

You have
1 minute to try.

A-Minute-A-Day – Debrich Publishing – Copyright 2019

Practice every day.   Put your score on the back.

17

Sweet Shop

Mrs Smith needs to order more sweets for her shop.

Can you help her by telling her how many sweets are in each jar?

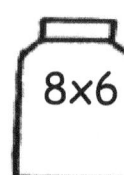

6x6	3x6	5x6	8x6	4x6	7x6
9x6	6x6	10x6	2x6	5x6	9x6
4x6	1x6	7x6	3x6	0x6	8x6
2x6	5x6	8x6	0x6	10x6	6x6
4x6	3x6	7x6	10x6	2x6	9x6

You have 1 minute to try.
Practice every day. Write your score on the back.

18

Crocodile

The crocodile will reach the bank in 1 minute.
Can you get there before him?

You may only step on a stone if you can answer the question

Practice every day. Write your score on the back.

9x7

3x7

5x7

3x7

7x7

0x7

6x7

8x7

4x7

9x7

2x7

7x7

10x7

2x7

10x7

10x7

0x7

4x7

5x7

1x7

8x7

2x7

9x7

4x7

7x7

3x7

6x7

6x7

8x7

5x7

Start

A-Minute-A-Day - Debrich Publishing - Copyright 2019

Lighthouse

A-Minute-A-Day - Debrich Publishing - Copyright 2019

4x8
8x8
6x8
2x8
7x8
4x8
3x8
2x8
10x8
5x8
7x8
3x8
9x8
10x8
8x8
5x8
0x8
9x8
6x8
3x8
1x8
2x8
9x8
6x8
4x8
10x8
8x8
6x8
7x8
5x8

It is almost dark.

The lighthouse keeper must switch on the light quickly but he has dropped his key.

Can you take it to him?
You have just 1 minute to try.

Do not miss any questions

Practice every day. Write your score on the back.   20

Umbrellas

It is starting to rain.
You will need an umbrella.
You may only choose one if you know the answers.

Can you find all the answers in 1 minute?

8x9 Start

4x9

7x9

2x9

5x9   1x9   5x9   10x9

8x9   3x9

3x9   2x9   0x9

7x9   4x9   6x9   9x9

5x9   3x9   6x9

10x9   7x9   10x9

4x9   9x9

6x9   9x9   2x9   8x9   4x9

A-Minute-A-Day – Debrich Publishing – Copyright 2019

Practice every day.   Write your score on the back.   21

Ski Race

You have 1 minute to reach the winning post. but you must answer each question as you pass.

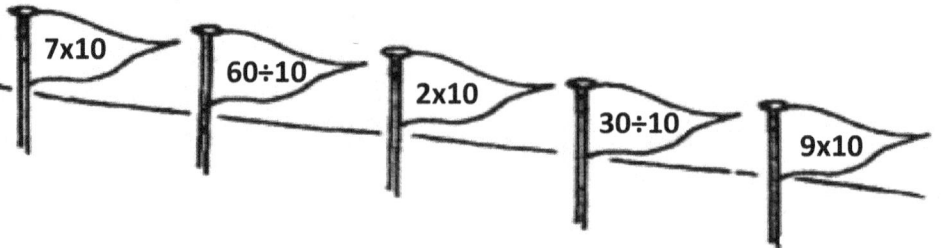

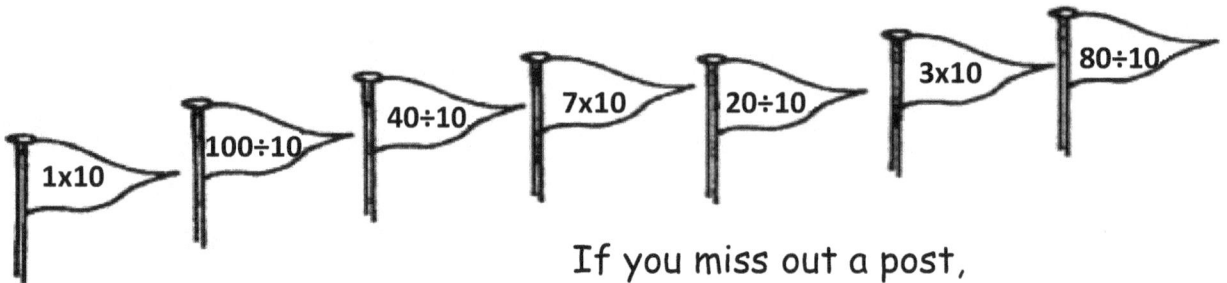

7x10

60÷10

2x10

30÷10

9x10

80÷10

3x10

20÷10

7x10

40÷10

100÷10

1x10

If you miss out a post, you must begin again!

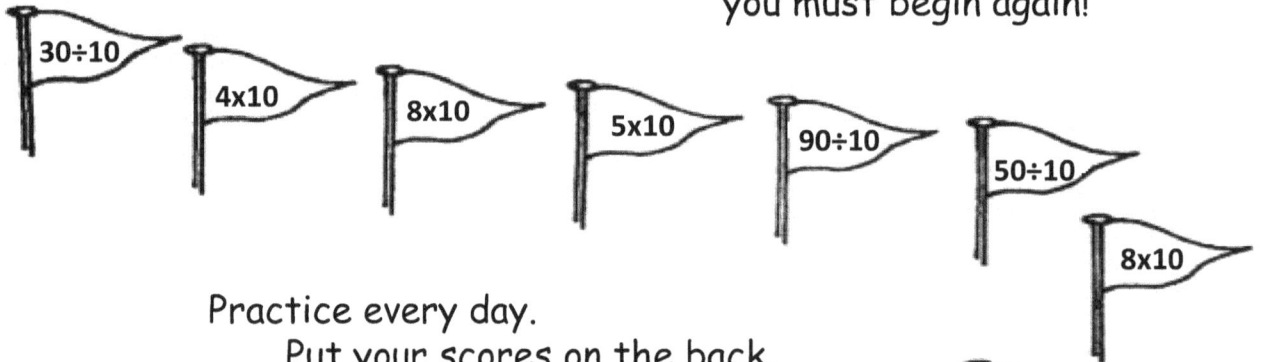

30÷10

4x10

8x10

5x10

90÷10

50÷10

8x10

80÷10

Practice every day.
Put your scores on the back.

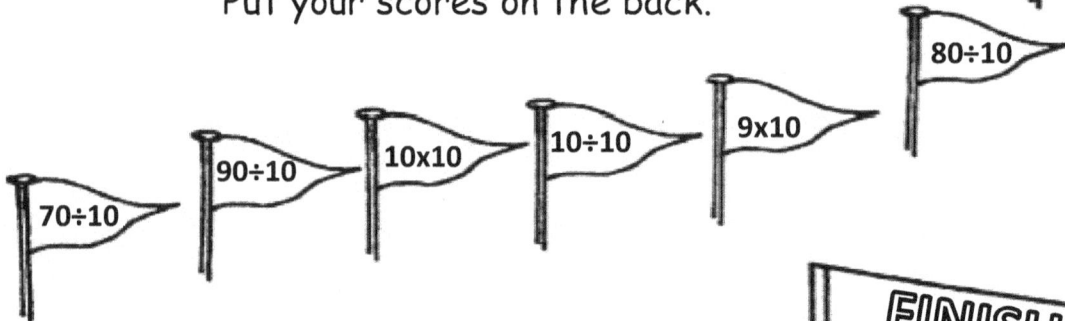

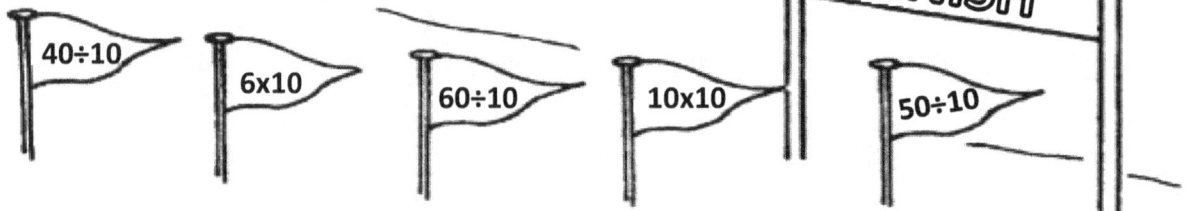

9x10

10÷10

10x10

90÷10

70÷10

FINISH

40÷10

6x10

60÷10

10x10

50÷10

22

Mary

"Mary, Mary, quite contrary .... "

Mary can guess the answer
to every question in 1 minute.
Can you beat her?

4 ÷ 2

20 ÷ 2

14 ÷ 2

10 ÷ 2

8 ÷ 2
Start

16 ÷ 2

8 ÷ 2

10 ÷ 2

18 ÷ 2

6 ÷ 2

16 ÷ 2

12 ÷ 2

6 ÷ 2

20 ÷ 2

8 ÷ 2

14 ÷ 2

4 ÷ 2

18 ÷ 2

6 ÷ 2

18 ÷ 2

14 ÷ 2

10 ÷ 2

20 ÷ 2

2 ÷ 2

12 ÷ 2

4 ÷ 2

12 ÷ 2

8 ÷ 2

20 ÷ 2

16 ÷ 2

Well done !!!

Practice every day. Write your score on the back

A-Minute-A-Day - Debrich Publishing - Copyright 2019

Sam's father is going to buy him
a tank and six fish.
Which tank will he choose?

Fish

Can you say how many fish are in each tank?
See if you can count them all in 1 minute.

Start

27 ÷ 3	3 ÷ 3	30 ÷ 3	12 ÷ 3	21 ÷ 3
9 ÷ 3	24 ÷ 3	12 ÷ 3	6 ÷ 3	15 ÷ 3
12 ÷ 3	9 ÷ 3	3 ÷ 3	27 ÷ 3	21 ÷ 3
15 ÷ 3	24 ÷ 3	27 ÷ 3	30 ÷ 3	6 ÷ 3
3 ÷ 3	30 ÷ 3	18 ÷ 3	12÷3	24÷3
21 ÷ 3	9 ÷ 3	27 ÷ 3	6 ÷ 3	15 ÷ 3

Practice every day.   Write your score on the back.   24

Plums

"Little Jack Horner
sat in a corner ...."

Jack is looking for a pie
with lots of plums inside.
Can you tell him how many
plums are in each pie?

36 ÷ 4   24 ÷ 4   12 ÷ 4   40 ÷ 4   4 ÷ 4   28 ÷ 4

20 ÷ 4   24 ÷ 4   36 ÷ 4   8 ÷ 4   32 ÷ 4   16 ÷ 4

12 ÷ 4   32 ÷ 4   20 ÷ 4   24 ÷ 4   40 ÷ 4   8 ÷ 4

24 ÷ 4   16 ÷ 4   28 ÷ 4   4 ÷ 4   36 ÷ 4   28 ÷ 4

16 ÷ 4   40 ÷ 4   4 ÷ 4   32 ÷ 4   8 ÷ 4   20 ÷ 4

Practice every day. Write your score on the back.

Homework

John must finish his homework
before the school bus arrives.
Can you help him?
Hurry! The bus will be here
in 1 minute.

35 ÷ 5

50 ÷ 5

30 ÷ 5

40 ÷ 5

25 ÷ 5

start

5 ÷ 5

15 ÷ 5

15 ÷ 5

45 ÷ 5

45 ÷ 5

5 ÷ 5

20 ÷ 5

10 ÷ 5

35 ÷ 5

25 ÷ 5

50 ÷ 5

10 ÷ 5

30 ÷ 5

5 ÷ 5

40 ÷ 5

20 ÷ 5

45÷ 5

50 ÷ 5

30÷ 5

15 ÷ 5

10 ÷ 5

35 ÷ 5

20 ÷ 5

25 ÷ 5

40 ÷ 5

Practice every day.
Write your score on the back.

26

Tunnel

Can you guess how many people are in each carriage?

$18 \div 6$ $60 \div 6$ $24 \div 6$ $42 \div 6$ $30 \div 6$

Finish

$54 \div 6$

$60 \div 6$ $24 \div 6$ $48 \div 6$ $6 \div 6$ $36 \div 6$

$12 \div 6$

$42 \div 6$ $6 \div 6$ $30 \div 6$ $18 \div 6$ $36 \div 6$ $48 \div 6$

Hurry! In 1 minute, the train will disappear into the tunnel.

$24 \div 6$

$30 \div 6$ $42 \div 6$ $6 \div 6$ $54 \div 6$ $12 \div 6$

$60 \div 6$

$36 \div 6$ $12 \div 6$ $48 \div 6$ $18 \div 6$ $54 \div 6$

Start

Practice every day.   Write your score on the back.   27

Socks

Mum has washed the socks, but they are in a muddle.
Can you put them in pairs again?

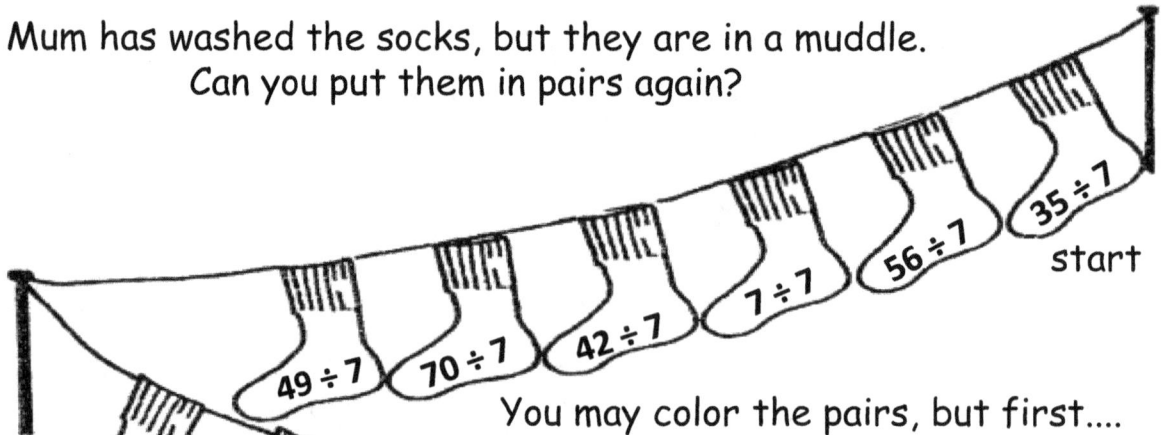

start

$35 \div 7$

$56 \div 7$

$7 \div 7$

$42 \div 7$

$70 \div 7$

$49 \div 7$

You may color the pairs, but first....
you must answer the questions.

$14 \div 7$

$63 \div 7$

$21 \div 7$

$56 \div 7$

$70 \div 7$

$42 \div 7$

You have 1 minute to try

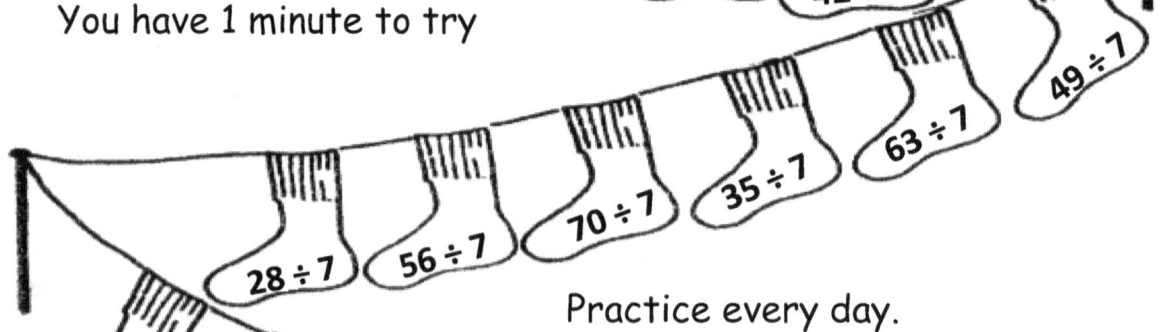

$49 \div 7$

$63 \div 7$

$35 \div 7$

$70 \div 7$

$56 \div 7$

$28 \div 7$

Practice every day.

$49 \div 7$

$14 \div 7$

$63 \div 7$

$42 \div 7$

$28 \div 7$

$7 \div 7$

$42 \div 7$

Write your score on the back.

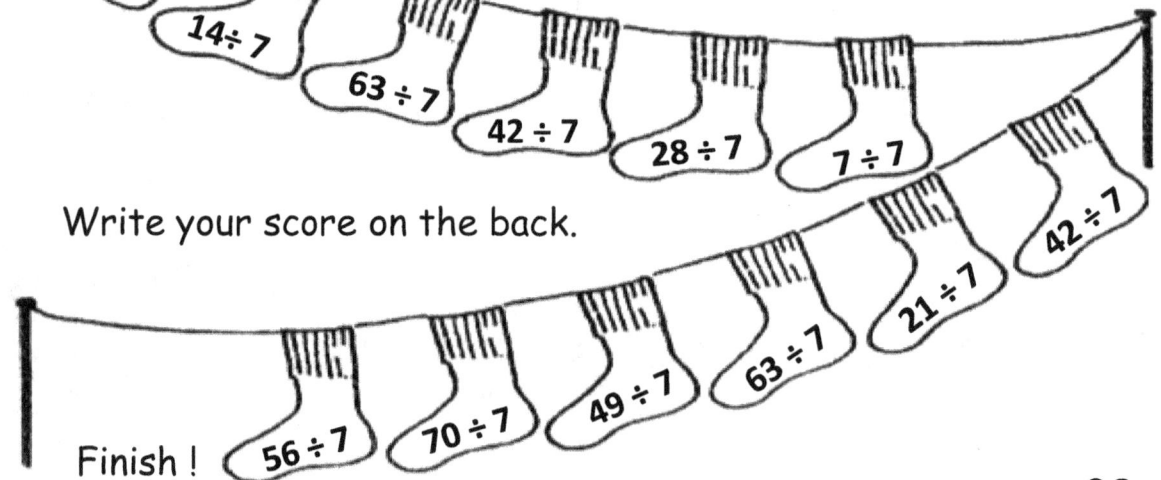

$21 \div 7$

$63 \div 7$

$49 \div 7$

$70 \div 7$

$56 \div 7$

Finish !

Eggs

Each day, Mrs Jones collects her eggs in a basket.
Can you help her to count them?

start

32÷8

48÷8

8÷8

80÷8

40÷8

24÷8

48÷8

72÷8

32÷8

16÷8

64÷8

16÷8

72÷8

24÷8

56÷8

8÷8

56÷8

16÷8

72÷8

32÷8

40÷8

64÷8

80÷8

40÷8

80÷8

8÷8

24÷8

56÷8

48÷8

64÷8

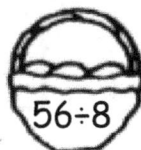

Practice every day. Write your score on the back. 29

A-Minute-A-Day - Debrich Publishing - Copyright 2019

Bins

Somebody has mixed up the refuse bins.....
Can you help the men to take
them back to the right houses?

start

You have 1 minute to find all the answers.

Practice every day.

Write your score on the back.

Finish

Time

All the clocks are set at "half past" or "o'clock"

Can you tell the time on them all in just 1 minute?

Start

Finish

A-Minute-A-Day - Debrich Publishing - Copyright 2019

Practice every day

Write your scores on the back.

31

Alarm

In 1 minute, the alarm will ring.
Can you tell the time on every clock
before it does?

start

finish

Practice every day.

Write your score on the back.

32

Watch

Peter's uncle has given him a watch.
He is learning to tell the time.

Can you help him by telling him the time
on all these watches?

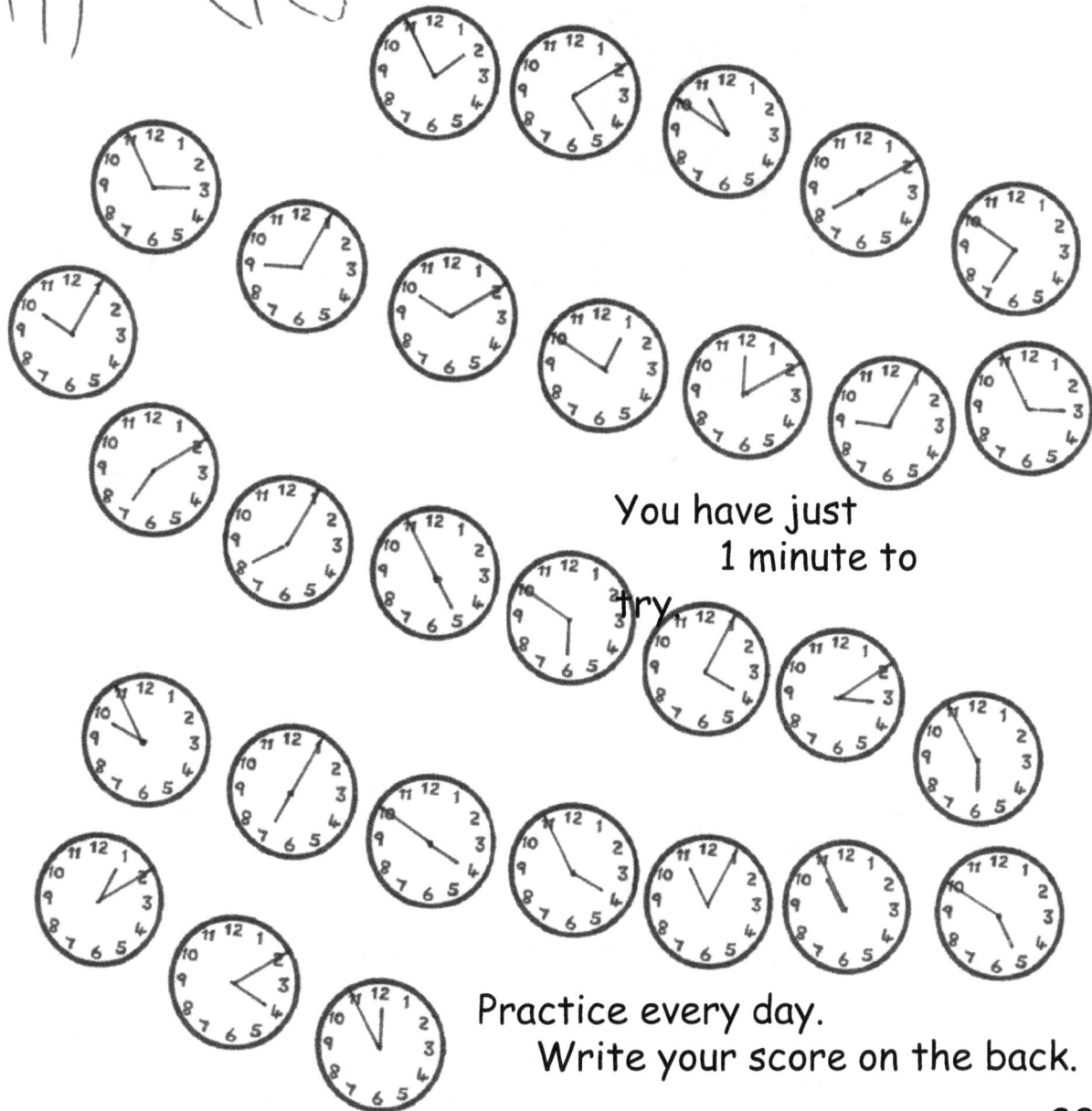

You have just
1 minute to
try.

Practice every day.
Write your score on the back.

Meg

Meg has just learned to tell the time.
She can read the times on all these clocks in just 1 minute.
Can you beat her?

start

Practice every day.

Write your scores on the back.

Well
done!

34

Snack

The children have brought snack money to school.

Can you count how much each child has brought?

Hurry!

The bell will ring for break in 1 minute.

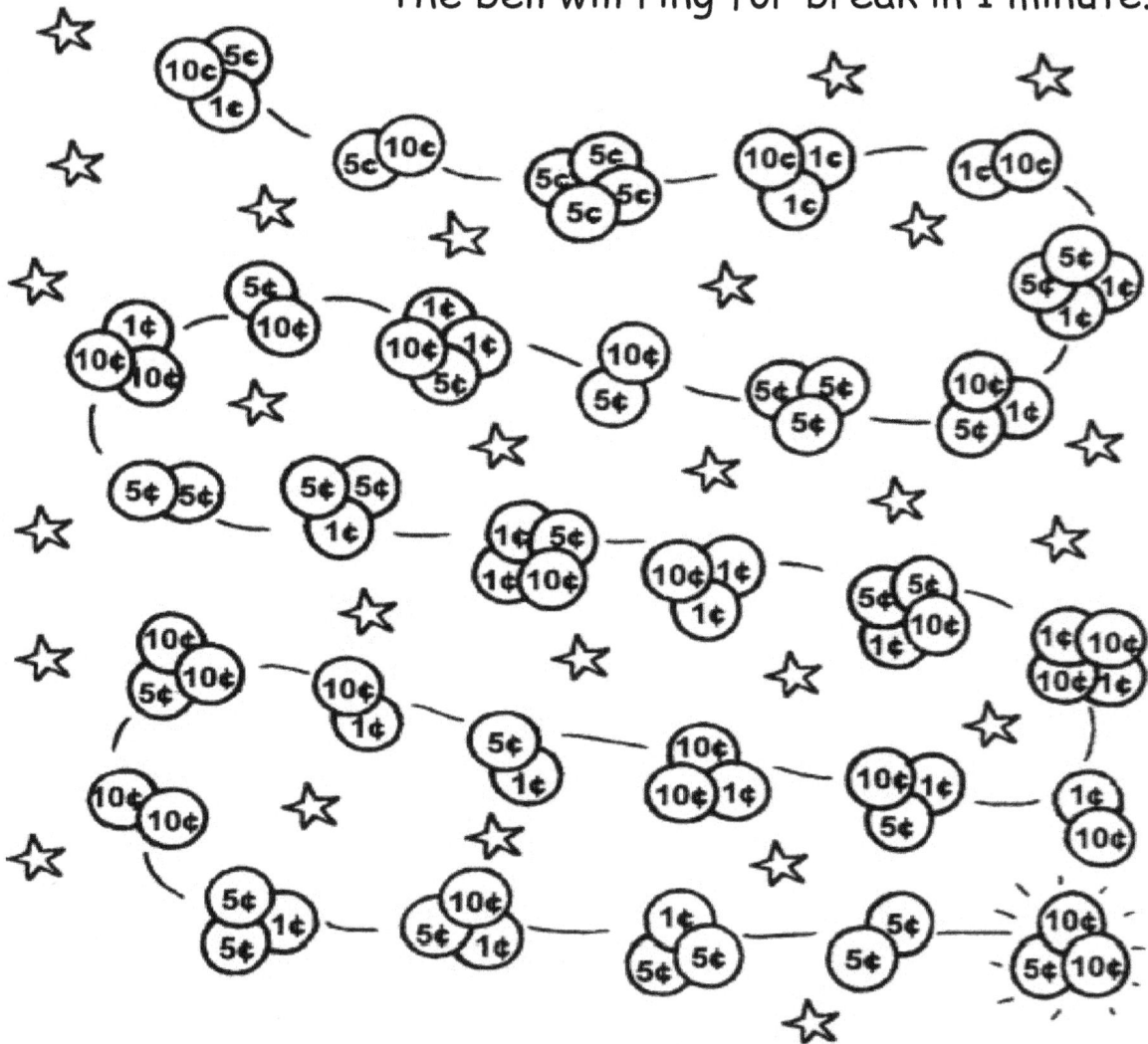

Practice every day.   Write your score on the back.   35

Piggy Bank

The children have been saving up.
Can you count how much each one has saved?

5¢ 5¢   5¢ 5¢   10¢   25¢   5¢ 10¢
1¢ 1¢   10¢ 10¢   5¢ 5¢
   25¢   10¢

10¢   5¢   10¢
5¢ 1¢   10¢ 5¢   1¢ 25¢

5¢   5¢   25¢
5¢ 10¢   25¢ 10¢   25¢

1¢   5¢   25¢
10¢   5¢ 10¢ 1¢ 1¢   10¢ 1¢
         10¢   1¢ 1¢

You have 1 minute to try

                                                5¢ 5¢
                                                 25¢

25¢   25¢   10¢ 10¢
5¢ 1¢   10¢ 10¢   1¢ 10¢   5¢ 5¢   10c
                        1¢   5¢

1¢
5¢ 5¢

Practice every day

1¢   10¢   1¢
25¢ 1¢   25¢   10¢ 10¢   25¢ 5¢
          10¢ 25¢   5¢ 5¢
10¢ 1¢   10¢
   5¢

                                    25¢ 10¢
                                      5¢

Write your score on the back

36

A-Minute-A-Day - Debrich Publishing - Copyright 2019

School Outing

The children are going on an outing.
They have all brought spending money.

Can you help them to count it before they set off?
Hurry! The bus leaves in 1 minute.

A-Minute-A-Day – Debrich Publishing – Copyright 2019

Practice every day. Write your score on the back 37

Change

The children have stopped to buy candy on the way to school. They each have 25¢.

Can you help the storekeeper give them the correct change?

Hurry! School begins in 1 minute.

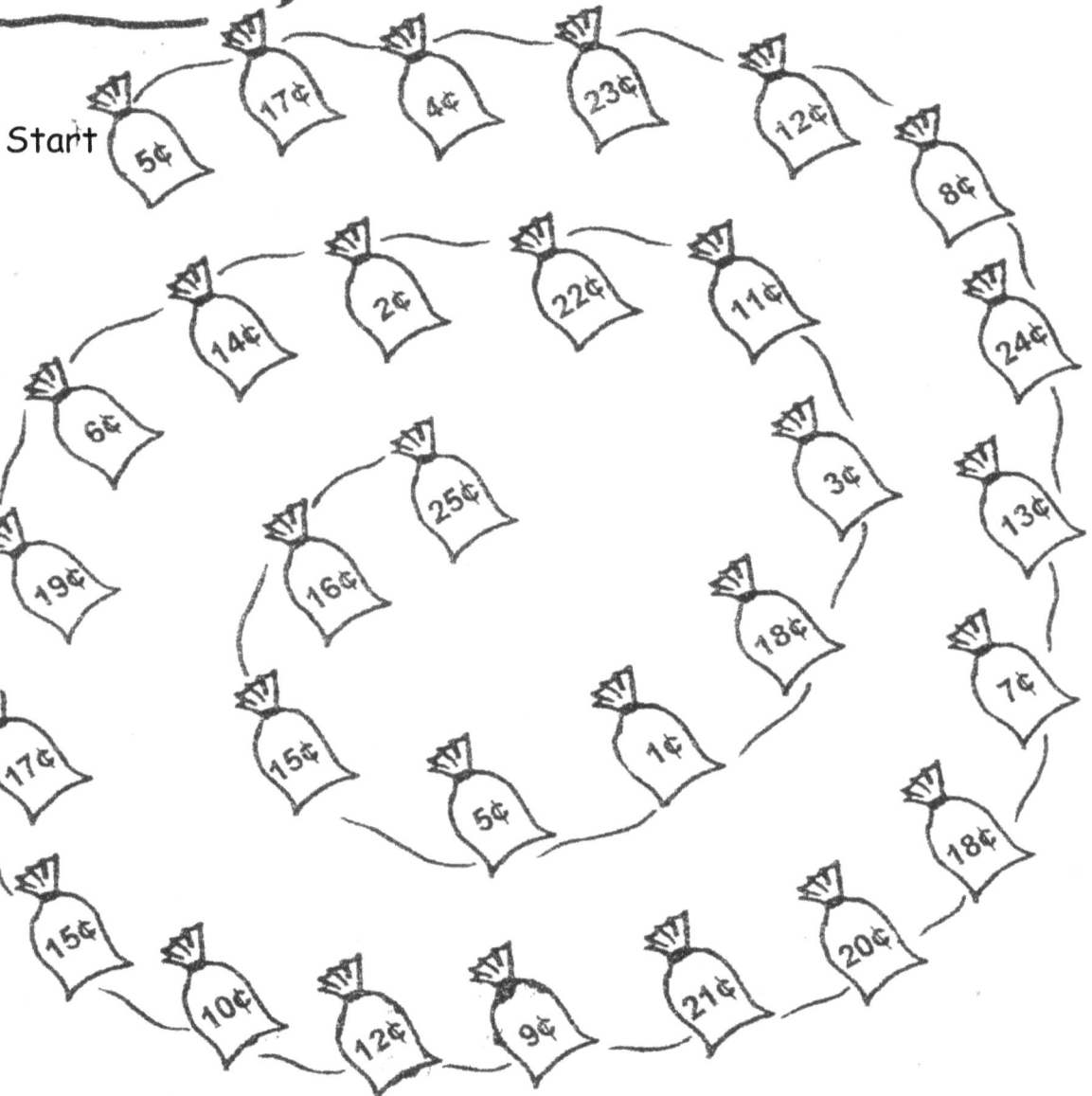

Start

5¢   17¢   4¢   23¢   12¢   8¢

14¢   2¢   22¢   11¢   24¢

6¢   25¢   3¢   13¢

19¢   16¢   18¢   7¢

17¢   15¢   1¢

15¢   5¢   18¢

10¢   12¢   9¢   21¢   20¢

Practice every day.   Write your score on the back

Spends

Sally has 50¢ to buy a toy .
She does not want to spend it all.

Each toy has a price tag.

Can you help her decide which to
choose by telling her how much
change she would have?

20¢ 42¢ 30¢ 12¢ 37¢ 29¢ 24¢

Start

33¢ 10¢ 16¢ 48¢ 49¢

27¢ 26¢ 15¢

You have just 1 minute to try 34¢ 22¢

47¢ 39¢ 40¢ 29¢ 36¢

35¢

18¢ 32¢ 8¢ 5¢ 14¢ 45¢ 25¢

Practice every day.   Write your scores on the back.   39

Snakes and Ladders

Can you climb all the ladders in 1 minute without a mistake?

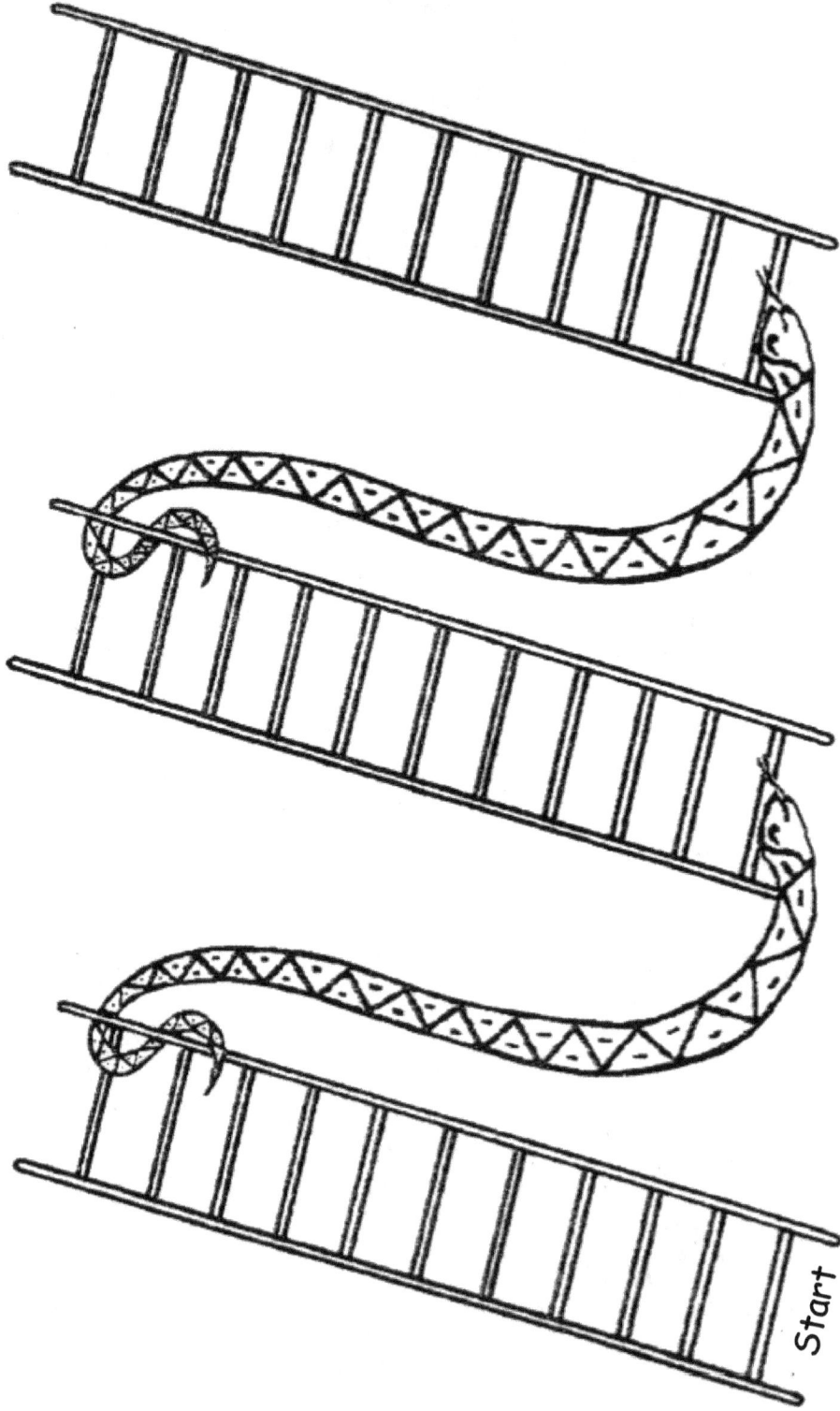

Start

Practice every day.

Write your score on the back.

Skyscraper

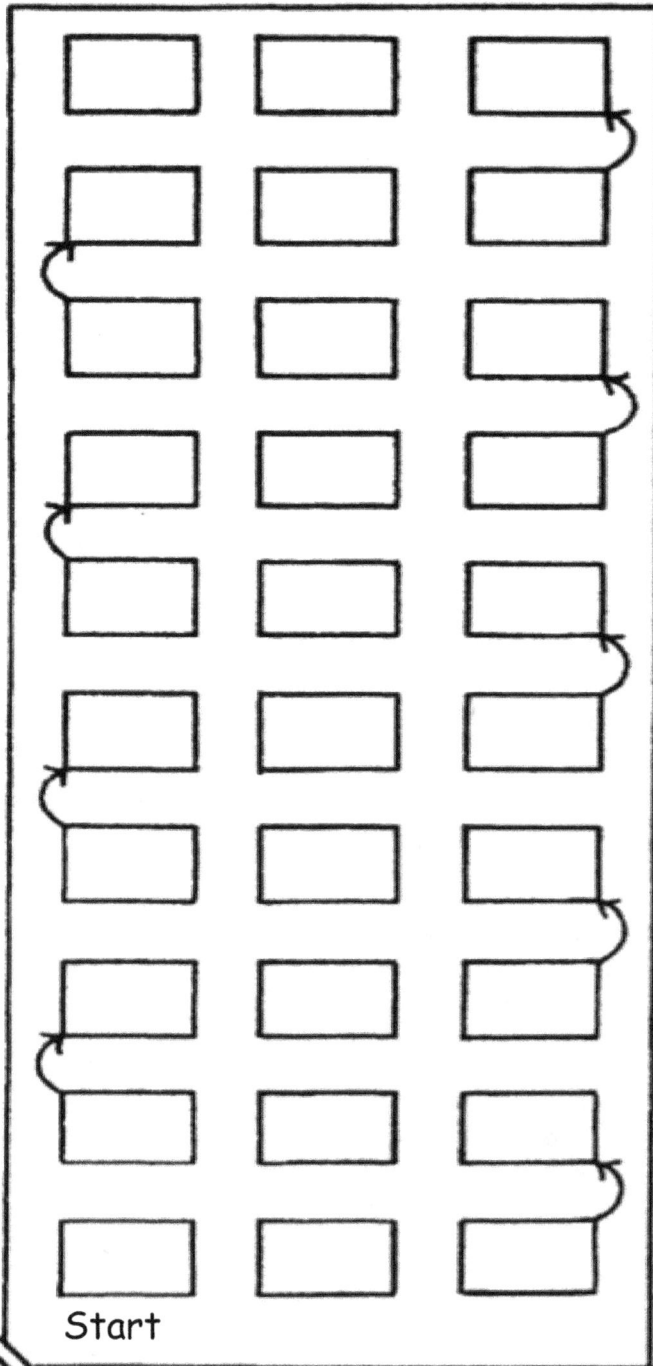

Can you light up the building in 1 minute?

You may only color a window if you can answer the question.

Do not miss out any questions!

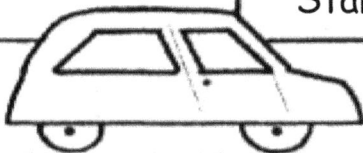

Start

A-Minute-A-Day Mental Maths [US]
RECORD SHEET

Name :- _____

	Date Commenced	Date Completed	Comments
1 Counting objects up to 6			
2 Counting objects up to 10			
3 Counting objects up to 12			
4 Number recognition up to 11			
5 Number recognition up to 20			
6 Number recognition up to 30			
7 Addition up to 10			
8 Addition up to 20			
9 Subtraction from 7			
10 Subtraction from 10			
11 Subtraction from 20			
12 Subtraction between 0 and 10			
13 Subtraction between 10 and 20			
14 Multiplying by 2			
15 Multiplying by 3			
16 Multiplying by 4			
17 Multiplying by 5			
18 Multiplying by 6			
19 Multiplying by 7			
20 Multiplying by 8			
21 Multiplying by 9			
22 Multiplying & Dividing by 10			
23 Dividing by 2			
24 Dividing by 3			
25 Dividing by 4			
26 Dividing by 5			
27 Dividing by 6			
28 Dividing by 7			
29 Dividing by 8			
30 Dividing by 9			

A-Minute-A-Day Maths

RECORD SHEET (continued)

Name :- _____

	Date Commenced	Date Completed	Comments
31 O'clock/half past			
32 Quarter to/quarter past			
33 5 to/5 past, 10to/10past			
34 20 to/20 past, 25to/25past			
35 Addition up to 25c			
36 Addition up to 50c			
37 Addition up to $1			
38 Change from 25c			
39 Change from 50c			
40			
41			
42			

"A-MINUTE-A-DAY" MENTAL MATHS

Dear _____

I am writing to ask for your help with the work _____ is bringing home from school today.

It relates directly to the stage (s)he is focusing upon at school.

A *maximum* of 15 minutes each day is all that you will need……..about ten minutes to practice and one minute to test, in a room free from distractions such as TV, toys etc.

Do not worry if your child's score is low at the beginning - the emphasis is on *improvement*, i.e. if the score is 6 one night, aim for 8 the next and so on.

Above all……keep the session *brief, light-hearted* and remember to give *lots of praise* for effort.

Would you please write your child's score on the back of the sheet and return it to school every day. Thank you.

Signed ....

"A-MINUTE-A-DAY" MENTAL MATHS

Dear _____

I am writing to ask for your help with the work _____ is bringing home from school today.

It relates directly to the stage (s)he is focusing upon at school.

A *maximum* of 15 minutes each day is all that you will need…….about ten minutes to practice and one minute to test, in a room free from distractions such as TV, toys etc.

Do not worry if your child's score is low at the beginning - the emphasis is on *improvement*, i.e. if the score is 6 one night, aim for 8 the next and so on.

Above all……keep the session *brief, light-hearted* and remember to give *lots of praise* for effort.

Would you please write your child's score on the back of the sheet and return it to school every day. Thank you.

Signed ....